DAVID ROBERTS

A journey in Egypt

Commentary on drawings by David Roberts: Rita Bianucci

© Copyright 1997 by Casa Editrice Bonechi, via Cairoli 18/b - 50131 Florence - Italy
Tel. 55/576841 - Fax 55/5000766
E-mail: bonechi@bonechi.it
Internet: www.bonechi.it

Printed in Italy by Centro Stampa Editoriale Bonechi
Translation by Kate Parenti

ISBN 88-8029-110-6

* * *

INTRODUCTION

David Roberts was neither the first nor the only artist to travel in the Middle East bringing back drawings of the places and peoples he had seen, but he is certainly the most famous. He was born in Edinburgh in 1796 into a humble family. His father was a cobbler, and he himself started to work at a very young age. By the time he was eight he was already a painter, specialised in the imitation of marble and wood. Even after he obtained a post as a scene-painter in Scotland he continued to practice his old trade in the periods in which the theatre did not require his work. Subsequently, he was employed full time in the theatres of Glasgow, Edinburgh and, from 1822, London, where he worked for the famous opera-house at Covent Garden. At the same time Roberts started to exhibit water-colours and oil-paintings, as well as illustrating books with his sketches, gaining praise from the critics and enjoying fair commercial success.

In the years from 1824 to 1830, he travelled in France, Belgium, Holland and Germany. In 1832-33 he spent 11 months in Spain, visiting the north, Madrid, and then proceeding down to Granada, Cordova and Gibraltar. From there he crossed over to Marocco, leaving the European continent for the first time. He then visited Seville, remaining there for five months.

During his stay abroad he produced drawings and oil paintings, and once back home, he illustrated four issues of "The Landscape Annual" and published 27 lithographic prints in "Roberts' Picturesque Sketches of Spain".

His work was well received and the numerous Spanish subjects that he produced in the following years were sold with no difficulty. With the money earned in this way he organised his tour in the East.

Thus, in 1838-9, he spent 11 months travelling in Egypt, Syria and the Holy Land. After his return home, he was elected as a member of the Royal Academy (1841) and the year after, he started to publish the drawings made during his tour, monthly, in collaboration with the lithographer Louis Haghe. These drawings made him famous in Britain and elsewhere.

In 1843, he was once again travelling through Europe and ten years later (1853-54) he spent six months in Rome and Naples. When he died, on the 25th November 1864, the humble painter was a famous man whose customers were rich businessmen and noblemen; even Queen Victoria and Prince Albert commissioned work from him and he himself visited the court on several occasions in order to discuss it. Roberts' fame is due to his ability in architectural drawings and those of monuments, but he also painted scenes from daily life. He was fascinated by the ruins left by men of past ages and returned many times to the same place, drawing his subject from various view points and at different hours, taking care to catch the variations in the light at different moments in the day. His works provide a precise, almost photographic, documentation of the appearance of ancient Egypt, now forever lost.

Alexandria: "Cleopatra's Needles"... - These obelisks have been called "Cleopatra's Needles" since the Middle Ages, even though they are in no way connected with the Egyptian queen. According to Pliny they stood before the Caesareum, the sanctuary in honour of the deified Emperor, which was started by Cleopatra and finished by Augustus.

The obelisks had originally been erected by Tuthmosis III on the occasion of the third jubilee of his reign to honour his "father" Re-Harakhty in Heliopolis, the seat of some of the most important religious organizations in the country. The ovals on the sides of the obelisks bear the names of Tuthmosis III and of the later Ramesses II, called the Great. They were transported to Alexandria in 10 BC by Augustus.

When Roberts arrived in Alexandria this is how he saw the two monolyths, as the earthquake of 1301 had left them: still intact, even though one had fallen.

The almost hazy appearance of the surrounding ruins backed by the glittering expanse of the sea contribute to create the atmosphere which envelops the monuments: an atmosphere of desolate decay, but at the same time of the proud affirmation of a past which defies death.

... and the "Pillar of Pompey" - The "Pillar of Pompey", made of red granite from Aswan like "Cleopatra's needles", is situated on high ground which allows it to stand out against the surrounding countryside. Its name, dating from the time of the Crusades, derives from it being erroneously believed to be the cenotaph of the general who was killed on Egyptian soil. In actual fact the pillar was part of the Serapeum, the Ptolemaic temple dedicated to the god Sarapis.

The foundations are made up of elements from much older monuments, as is testified for example by the name of Sethos I carved on one of the blocks. The capital is Corinthian and, as the hollow on top of it suggests, was probably intended to hold a statue.

An inscription on the pedestal informs us that the monument was re-erected in 292 AD by Publius, the Roman Prefect of Egypt, in honour of the Emperor Diocletian.

In the nineteenth century, the pillar was still a reference point for sailors, and travellers coming from the desert due to its high position and its size.

Cairo: the market - On visiting Cairo, Roberts could not help but feel the fascination that the Eastern world holds for travellers: the scenes from daily life which are so different from the West, the slave market, Islamic architecture; all this made just as great an impression on Roberts as the monuments of ancient Egypt. The market, with its colours, with its pungent smells, with the people lingering in front of this or that stall to appraise the wares or to bargain endlessly over prices, had always been and still is, a picturesque and compulsory stop for tourists.

Giza - Nineteenth century travellers could easily reach the zone of the pyramids if the level of the Nile was low and the intersecting canals dry and practicable: it took little more than an hour to journey from New to Old Cairo, cross the Nile on the ferry and finally reach the the village of Giza, from which the most famous group of pyramids in the world takes its name.
The journey became tortuous and much longer if the Nile was in flood and travel through the canals was no longer possible. The pyramids looked like this to Roberts from the East bank of the river: immense, despite their distance from the river, perfect forms rising out of the sands of the Libyan desert and projected into the sky. In front is the pyramid of Cheops, then that of Chephren, and lastly the pyramid of Mycerinus, all dating back to the Fourth Dynasty. Moved by the sight of them, the artist wrote: "What are the portentious works of Roman art in comparison with these...."

Cairo: Bab Zuweyla - *The bustling life near Bab el Mitwalli, today called Bab Zuweyla, the southernmost gate in the walls of the Fatimid city does not at all bring to mind a place of execution. And yet here in the heart of Old Cairo, from the Mameluke epoch onwards, capital sentences were carried out. The minarets which appear above the gateway are those of the Mu'ayyad Mosque, the Red Mosque, which flank the grand entrance on the outside.*

Giza: the pyramids of Cheops and Chefren - *Vast constructions in an absolutely empty landscape from which man seems almost to be banished, but by which he is also fascinated and attracted: the pyramid of Cheops stripped of its covering and without its point, that of Chephren, his son, the head of the Sphinx emerging out of the sand and the remains of other structures as far as the eye can see. All enveloped by the desert, and almost desert themselves.*
This is how the area of the pyramids appeared to travellers in in search of ancient ruins in Egypt last century: an arid realm of solitude in which the shade of a palm or a sycamore offered the only means of relief from the heat and fatigue.

9

Giza: the great Sphinx - *In his travel journal, Roberts admits to having been really struck by the dimensions of the pyramid of Cheops, or Great Pyramid, only when he started to climb it and that it was the Sphinx which aroused more powerful emotions in him.*

The enormous body buried in the sand waits once again, as it has had to wait many times before during its multi-millennial existence, to be dug clear in order to appear in its entirety to the eyes of men. Brought back to daylight already in the past by Amenhotep II and Tuthmosis IV, who under the Sphinx had dreams or visions which promised them sovreignty over the country if they freed it from the sand, it has suffered more than just the ravages of nature and the weather: the mutilated profile of the nose reminds us that the Sphinx was used as a target for the fire-arms of Mameluke soldiers during shooting practice.

Despite this, the sculpture continues to cast its mysterious spell. Even David Roberts, usually so precise in his drawings, seems not to have been immune to the enigmatic power to fascinate which emanates from that face, at least if we judge by the sketch in which a sand storm is about to break over the Sphinx and the groups of caravaneers who surround it: the positioning of the sun, Sphinx and pyramids is totally unreal, given the well-known fact that the Sphinx faces the East.

The necropolis of Beni Hasan - *The tombs of the Beni Hasan necropolis are cut in the rock face which runs along the right hand side of the Nile and were destined to hold the nomarchs of the Eleventh and Twelfth Dynasties. Several of them have characteristics which make them different from Egyptian building typology. The fluted columns tapering at the top, on which rests an abacus, as well as the decoration on the cornice above the architrave of the façade, call to mind the Doric style of the Greeks. Roberts notes that inside the tombs the walls are covered with the famous paintings showing the daily life and sports of ancient Egypt which were copied down by Champollion and others.*

Entrance to the Caves of Beni Hasan

Boat with slaves - *A boat glides over the calm waters of the Nile which seem to lap the pyramids of Dahshur, called the "Bent Pyramid" and the "Red Pyramid", and those of Saqqara; a boat like many others, but with a cargo of slaves.*
"...the slave boat (was)...owned by...a Greek who had the effrontery to tell me that he was a Christian...The trade must be profitable, since such a journey could be advantageously taken with eleven only of these poor wretches for the market...The Greek, in hopes of a customer, pointed out the best of them to me, and descanted on their points with the skill of a jockey. Some were modest and shy, others tittered and seemed much amused with my costume, a blouse and trousers not one-third the width of a Turk's. The best of these poor creatures was worth eighteen or twenty pounds sterling. I regreted that I had too few words of Arabic or Greek to tell the old rascal how much his occupation was abhorred in England."

Dendera: the Temple of Hathor - *The Temple of Hathor at Dendera is one of the best preserved and dates back to the Ptolemaic era. The vestibule in front of it is made up of six rows of four columns, crowned with splendid capitals adorned with cow-eared heads of the goddess Hathor surmounted by sistra, an attribute of divinity. The magnificence of the work, the extraordinary richness of the sculptural and pictorial decorations and above all the colours, at that time still so vivid that they seemed to have only just been laid on, fascinated Roberts who noted that everywhere was literally covered with hieroglyphics from top to bottom and from one end of the ceiling to the other, inside and outside and right up to the narrow stairway where the light of day is unable to penetrate. The symbols, he wrote, went from a height of 15 feet to those of such minute dimensions that a magnifying glass would be necessary in order to examine them.*

The work of digging the temple out of the sand had not yet been finished as we can see from the two drawings of the vestibule and that of one of the entrances to the sacred enclosure. Of the latter, only the upper part emerges, on which the sun's globe spreads its protective wings almost as if it wishes to extend its benevolence to the men who dawdle below.

Dendera Dec 7th 1838

David Roberts R.A.

The Temple of Hathor and the "mammisi" - *Another drawing in which the vestibule of the Temple of Hathor appears on the left and on the right we can see the lateral colonnade of the "mammisi" from the Roman era.*

In the "mammisi" or "birth-house" ritual ceremonies connected with the birth of Ihy, the son of Hathor and of Horus of Edfou were celebrated.

The Temple of Month at Medamud - *Here we can only see five columns of the portico of the Temple of Medamud, which was built by Ptolemy VII Evergete II and was dedicated to the falcon-headed war god Month.*

The two central columns which flanked the portal are distinguished from the remaining three in that they have a composite capital instead of one with a closed lotus shape.

The ruins of Luxor - *The feluccas which glide silently on the Nile and the men near the "shadufs" for drawing water on both banks of the river seem unaware of the spectacular ruins of Luxor which along with the white minaret of the Abu el-Haggag mosque, stand out on the horizon.*

The sacred zone of Karnak - *The rosy dawn light strikingly highlights the distinct features of the various buildings in the great complex of Ammon at Karnak. From left to right we can see distinctly, the first pylon, the column of Taharqa and the second pylon, immediately followed by the columns of the immense hypostyle hall, the obelisk of Tuthmosis I and that of Hatshepsut. On the extreme right lie the columns and pillars of the Festival Hall of Tuthmosis III and the gateway of Nectanebo.*

The hypostyle hall at Karnak - *Roberts was so over-awed when he saw the ruins of Karnak that he despaired of ever being able to express his feelings in his drawings. He wrote that it was so much more impressive than anything that he had seen up to that point that he was quite unable to paragon it with anything. He observed that a man looks like a pigmy next to the main columns which have a circumference of 35 feet, 6 inches and that the overturned blocks lying haphazardly around were so enormous that it was difficult to see how they could have been knocked down, let alone how it was ever possible to raise them.*

Roberts, however, was right: even if his drawings, with the little groups of men which appear in them, are able to convey an idea of the proportions of the buildings at Karnak, they have not the power to convey to us the emotion felt by Roberts and whoever else has been there in person.

The three drawings reproduced here show us the forest of columns of the hypostyle hall, seen from various angulations. It is virtually impossible to find an undecorated square centimetre: the architraves, the capitals, shaped like open or closed lotuses, the shafts of the columns, all surfaces are covered with inscriptions and reliefs. The colours, although dimed by the passage of the centuries, still give substance to the images created by the ancient Egyptian artisans.

The column of Taharqa - *This column which stands all alone was part, with another nine columns, of the colonnade erected by Pharoah Taharqa of the XXVth Dynasty. In the background, the great hypostyle hall and the ruins of the second pylon can be partially seen. The hypostyle hall's impressive forest of columns, which seems almost like a petrified wood of papyri, made a profound impression on Roberts who made numerous drawings of it from various different angles.*

Karnak, the Nile and, on the other side of the river, the city of the dead - *The sun has just set behind the rise of the west bank of the Nile, where the pharoahs and princes of the New Kingdom hewed their tombs out of the rock hoping to save them from the sacrilegious avidity of robbers. Even in ancient times the royal tombs attracted numerous plunderers, despite divine malediction of whosoever dared to violate them. These plunderers tore the mummies to pieces in order to steal the precious jewelry which accompanied the dead in their journey into the next world. On this side of the river, suffused by the golden light of the sun stands the city of the living, the "Thebes of a hundred doors" sung of by Homer, where innumerable Pharoahs in the succession of dynasties competed to leave evidence of the power and riches attained by the Country of Two Lands. Here pylons were raised, temples built and obelisks and monuments erected to honour the Theban triad: the great Ammon, the invisible god, "king of kings", his consort Mut and his son Khonsu. The generations of men who built these marvels have vanished into nothing, the multitudes of priests who officiated in the temples have also disappeared, the merchants and boatmen who thronged the quays along the Nile are no longer there, but these solitary ruins are still able to transmit their message of power and glory to whoever approaches them.*

Luxor: the colossi of Ramesses II and the remaining obelisk - *Roberts saw only one of the two obelisks in red granite which had originally been erected in front of the pylon constructed by Ramesses II. A few years before his journey in Egypt, the missing obelisk had been transported to Paris and set up in the present day Place de la Concorde (1835-36). Two colossal seated statues flank the entrance to the great court. They are still buried up to the chest and are, as Roberts notes, sadly disfigured as is everything within reach of a hammer.*
The man who we see seated on a stool intent on drawing is David Roberts who sometimes liked to portray himself in his sketches.

The great pylon of Luxor - *The great pylon, like the other ancient monuments of Luxor, is surrounded by the mud houses of the inhabitants of the place, the structure of which is reminiscent of that of the pyramids. The large quantity of reddish clay vases to be seen on the flat roofs of the houses are nothing but pigeon-cotes.*
On the top of the obelisk a falcon appears to be waiting to swoop down on one of the many pigeons which fly to and from, from and to the vases in which they have built their nests.
On the left behind the pylon, on whose towers the Battle of Qadesh fought by Ramesses II against the Hittites is celebrated, emerges the summit of the minaret, which Roberts describes as being afflicted with all the pain in the world in order to rise to the height of the enormous pylon, whilst, he continues, the obelisk, carved out of a single block, vanishes above it like the work of a god.

Grand Entrance to the Temple of

of Two Colossal Statues of Ramses III Entrance to the Temple of Luxor

The disfigured colossus of Ramesses II - *The colossal statue of Ramesses II emerges from the accumulation of sand and rubble deposited in the course of centuries. On the top of the terribly disfigured head rests the double crown of Upper and Lower Egypt.*

General view of Luxor - *Called simply Nut, "the City", by the Egyptians, the ancient Thebes included both Karnak and Luxor. The latter occupied the southernmost part and was also the setting for majestic temples.*
In succession along the east bank of the Nile stand the obelisk of Ramesses II, then the great pylon of entry to the temple, immediately followed by the white minaret of the mosque of Abu el-Haggag, a venerated Muslim saint; beyond the sails of the felucca in the foreground, the magnificent colonnade of Amenhotep III reveals itself, followed by the ruins of the court in front of the actual temple.
Among the mighty ruins, life continues: the wretched white houses of the inhabitants, made from Nile mud, crowd close to one another and craft of various types and sizes sail on the river.

The Ramesseum and the colossi of Memnon - *Opposite ancient Thebes, on the other bank of the Nile, lies the city of the dead. Here the Pharoahs raised their mortuary temples, and, on the other side of the hills, their tombs were dug. Here we can see four Osiris pillars from the mortuary temple of Ramesses II, the Ramesseum, also called the Memnonium. The pillars portray the Pharoah in the shape of the mummified god Osiris, the god of the dead and the after life. These statues of Amenhotep III, the colossi of Memnon, have been mute witnesses of the daily rising of the sun for more than three thousand years. Set there to guard his mortuary temple, they emerge from the waters of the annual inundation of the Nile.*

28

Dayr el Medineh – Thebes.

David Roberts, R.A.

The Temples of Deir el - Medina and of Sethos I at Qurna - *A small group of people watch an artist at work with interest: maybe Roberts himself dressed "Turkish style" in conformity with the custom in Egypt last century. The scene is set inside the little temple that Ptolemy IV erected at Deir el-Medina, the village where the workers from the royal necropolis of Thebes lived.*

The ruins of the mortuary temple of Sethos I at Qurna were used by Roberts as the background for this group of people gathered round a water-pipe. The central seated figure is an officer of the Pacha and on his left is the Sheik of the village. The only woman present is wearing a long veil and characteristic face mask which conceals the whole face, leaving only the eyes uncovered.

The vestibule of the Temple of Esna - *The Ptolemaic Temple of Esna, of which all that remains is the vestibule with 24 columns, is much lower than ground level due to the stratification of debris. Last century one could only reach the hypostyle hall by going down a flight of steps. Dedicated to Khnum, the ram-headed god, it brings to mind, with its splendid composite capitals and its astronomical symbols, the vestibule of the temple of Dendera.*

The Temple of Horus at Edfou - *The Temple of Horus at Edfou is positioned on land higher than that of the Nile valley and it was started by Ptolemy III Evergete I in 237 BC.*
Although it was still semi-buried in the sand and had village huts nestling on its roof and in front of the pylon, it made a great impression on Roberts who noted in his journal that he found himself looking at the most beautiful temple of Egypt which, although not as big as that of Karnak and not so well preserved as that of Dendera, possessed all that one could desire.

The portico of the Temple of Edfou - *From the sand emerges the upper part of the majestic columns of the portico of the temple of Edfou. Magnificent capitals in different shaped pairs hold up the massive architrave with its carved decorations and its winged sun's globe, all of which serves as a base for the simple huts of the village. And yet nothing seems to detract from the beauty and dignity of this masterpiece.*

Edfou: the pylon and the portico - Once again we see the portico of the
temple with the pylon (second in size only to the first pylon of Karnak) in the
background. The extent to which the buildings are buried is such that several
people have been able to comfortably install themselves on top of the columns of
the portal leading into the hypostyle hall. Roberts wrote "Though half buried it
is more beautiful than if laid open, and reminds me of Piranesi etchings of the
Forum of Rome...". He went on to say that he was inclined to believe that if it
was cleared, this temple would reveal itself as the most complete after that of
Dendera.
The excavation work done by Mariette has shown that he was right.

The Nile at Gebel el-Silsila ... - *Shaduf at work and feluccas with sails unfurled to pick up the slightest breath of wind; in the background, the sandstone quarries. This is Gebel el-Silsila where the Nile flows through a narrow channel. For centuries the rock faces on both banks of the river were used as a source of material for the constructions of the New Kingdom Pharoahs.*
On the western bank, the outline of a strange mushroom-formed rock can be seen: the ancient quarrymen extracted the surrounding rock leaving it like that, a solitary witness of the labours of those who worked for the glory of the gods and of the Pharoahs.

... and at Aswan - *Another picture of the Nile, here at Aswan - in ancient times called Syene - with the island of Elephantine. "We walked over the ruins of this ancient city, which crowns the height of a rock jutting out into the stream. Nothing remains but the brick walls; so, after making a drawing of this part of the river, we crossed over to the island of Elephanta, where we found no vestiges of its ancient temples save a few columns and masses of rubbish. I saw one solitary figure with the arms folded on the breast, holding flagellum and crook; and on examining the wall next the stream I found it composed of stone covered with hieroglyphics, which must formerly have belonged to a temple."*

The sanctuary of Kom Ombo - *The great temple of Kom Ombo, dedicated to the crocodile-headed god Sobk and the falcon-headed Haroeris, revealed very little of its original structure as a double temple before excavation in 1893. What was visible however - the bright colours of the decoration, the richness of the carving, the elegance of the capitals - was enough to dazzle visitors. It is assailed by the desert sands on one side and, on the other, the waters of the Nile, which have done much damage. This fascinating edifice among "a few houses peeping above the sand is all that can be now seen of the once proud Ombros. Like its rival, Dendera, it is now desolate."*

Phila, Novʳ 18, 1838.

The island of Philae - *To travellers, drawn by its fame, and arriving there after having crossed endless burning expanses of sand and rock, the island of Philae must have seemed to be a real paradise. The boats were moored in a refreshing little bay, shaded by the green foliage of palms and sycamores and a little higher up were the pylons of the temple of Isis and the elegant Kiosk of Trajan.*

Philae had been a place of pilgrimage from ancient times because it was sacred to Isis, the consort of the good god Osiris who lay in eternal repose on the nearby island of Biga, access to which was prohibited to all human beings.

This drawing shows us the little island in all its loveliness, like a mirage of magical beauty in the desolate landscape which surrounds it.

In 1972-80, the entire complex of buildings, dating from the Ptolemaic era, was completely dismantled and accurately rebuilt on the nearby island of Agilkia, the conformation of which is similar to that of Philae, because of the construction of the High Dam on the Nile.

Philae: the Temple and the Kiosk of Trajan - *At the south end of the island, a vast court flanked with colonnades leads to the first pylon. Behind the central gateway we can glimpse the second pylon and on the extreme right appears the Kiosk of Trajan. This pavilion is one of the most beautiful monuments on Philae, despite the fact that its decoration was never completed. Of great elegance and harmony, it was reconstructed by the Emperor Trajan and has become the symbol of the island. It is made up of a single roofless rectangular room bounded by 14 columns, and the impression that it gave Roberts, as he records in his journal, was that the builders and sculptors had just left the site. He goes on to say that the sandstone is so light and the detail is so delicate and sharp that he found it difficult to grasp the fact that he was looking at a ruin two thousand years old.*

The Temple of Isis: the hypostyle hall - *In the small
hypostyle hall with eight pillars in front of the entrance portal to
the sanctuary of Isis, the colours of the paintings are still bright.
Roberts writes that he was amazed and enchanted by the elegance
of its proportions, but still more by the marvellous composition of
its colours which seemed to be only just laid on, and which, even
in the places where they had been exposed to sunlight, had
preserved their brightness.*
*On the ceiling, in a blue sky spangled with golden stars, we can
see the repeated figures of sacred beetle and vulture with wings
spread ; sacred boats "sail" on the structural elements of the
ceiling, under which the capitals bloom luxuriant; Pharoahs and
gods speak, by means of hieroglyphic inscriptions, from the
columns of the hall.*
*Not even the transformation of this hall in Coptic church in the
VIth century, at the time of Bishop Theodorus, was able to upset its
order or to impair its beauty: a few Greek crosses on the columns,
on a wall and on a broken altar is all that remains of the period in
which the Christian faith arrived here.*

A group of Nubians - *A group of Nubians with their peculiar hair-style pose for their portrait. Of the arms they carry, only the spears are part of their normal weaponry, the swords and shields are intended for selling.*

Abyssinian slaves and the Temple of Debod - *A group of Abyssinian slaves, mostly women, on their way to the slave market of Cairo rest under the shelter of a stunted palm tree; one of them is preparing their meal based on durra, Indian corn. In the background the Temple of Debod can be seen. This temple was completely dismantled in 1960 and presented to Spain as a sign of gratitude for its contribution to the campaign to save the temples of Nubia.*

The Temple of Kalabsha - *The mud houses of the village seem to press round the mighty walls of the Temple of Kalabsha, the ancient Talmis, for protection. This edifice is the largest temple in Nubia not hewed out of the rocks, and is dedicated to the Nubian sun god Marul, called Mandulis in Greek. It was built in the Ptolemaic era, on the site of an older building from the time of Amenhotep II, and later rebuilt and added to under Augustus. Roberts describes the approach to the temple as being a road of great square blocks which started at the river bank and led right up to a raised platform on to which the pylons flanking the great entrance faced.*

After the pylon, and beyond the court, in which the pillars that once surrounded it on three sides lie scattered, is the hypostyle hall, the façade of which has four columns still standing. Behind this lies the entrance to the sanctuary on top of which some huts can be seen.

In order to save it, the whole complex has been transferred to near the Aswan New Dam. Thus, unfortunately, it has lost its superb back-drop of harsh mountains towering behind it which rather than making it seem smaller, enhanced its grandeur.

Abu Simbel, as it was - *The most famous and impressive of the temples built by Ramesses II in Nubia are the rock ones of Abu Simbel on the West bank of the Nile. The smaller one is dedicated to his beautiful and very much loved wife Nefertari and the other is an astonishing glorification of Ramesses II himself. Never before had the wife of a Pharoah been portrayed on the façade of a temple with the same dimensions as the statues of her husband which flanked hers: an act of love on the part of Ramesses to the most loved of his wives, eternalised in stone in order that the memory of it would survive through the centuries.*

Abu Simbel: the temple -*Robert describes this temple, brought to light by the indefatigable Belzoni as being the more remarkable, though virtually engulfed by the desert sand. The sight of a double row of colossal statues of the Pharoah greets the astonished visitor who enters the bowels of the mountain: these appear* *to hold up the ceiling of the hall which is decorated with carvings and paintings of the victorious enterprises of Ramesses II. At a distance of three thousand years from the undertaking which had seen the face and heart of the mountain moulded into images of the Pharoah and his wife, the same architectural*

challenge presented itself once again. In a race against time whilst the water of the artificial lake rose much faster than expected, the two rock temples were cut into blocks and, with part of the surrounding rock, were transferred 90 metres higher and reassembled exactly as they had been originally. In February 1969 the "miracle of the sun" reoccured : its rays returned to pass through the whole length of the temple, penetrating the sanctuary and flooding the statues of Ammon, Harmakhis and the deified Pharoah with light. Only one statue remained untouched, that of Ptah, the god of darkness.

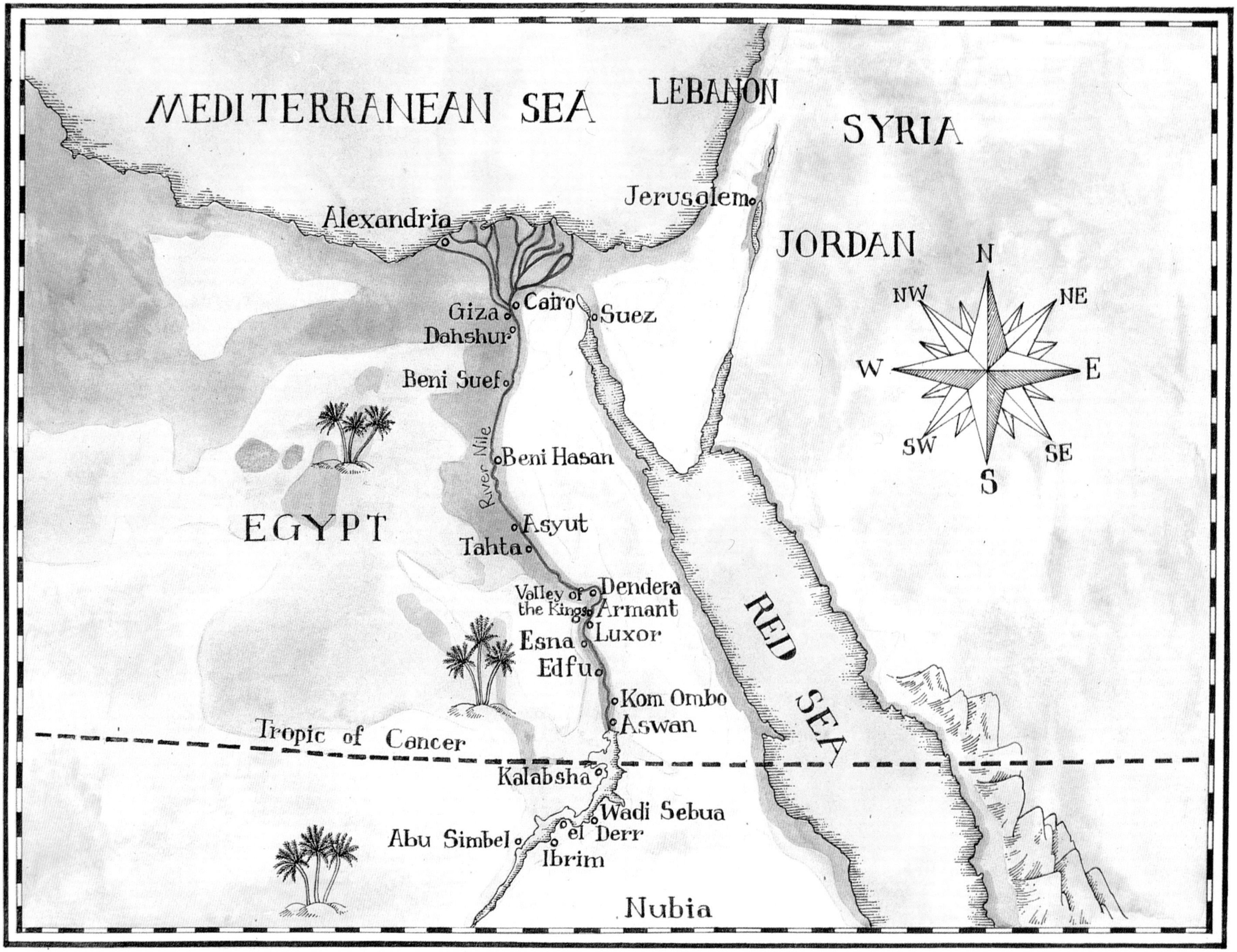
MEDITERRANEAN SEA
LEBANON
SYRIA
Jerusalem
JORDAN
Alexandria
Cairo
Giza
Suez
Dahshur
Beni Suef
River Nile
Beni Hasan
EGYPT
Asyut
Tahta
Valley of the Kings
Dendera
Armant
Luxor
Esna
Edfu
Kom Ombo
Aswan
Tropic of Cancer
RED SEA
Kalabsha
Wadi Sebua
el Derr
Abu Simbel
Ibrim
Nubia
N
NE
E
SE
S
SW
W
NW